William Tell

FRIEDRICH VON SCHILLER

Level 1

Retold by Nancy Taylor

Series Editors: Andy Hopkins and Jocelyn Potter

T0352429

Pearson Education Limited
Edinburgh Gate, Harlow,
Essex CM20 2JE, England
and Associated Companies throughout the world.

ISBN: 978-1-4082-3155-5

This edition first published by Pearson Education Ltd 2011

10

Text copyright © Pearson Education Ltd 2011
Illustrations by Pastiche Pastiche

Set in 11/14pt Bembo
Printed in China
SWTC/10

Published by Pearson Education Ltd

Every effort has been made to trace the copyright holders and we apologise in advance for any
unintentional omissions. We would be pleased to insert the appropriate acknowledgement in any
subsequent edition of this publication.

For a complete list of the titles available in the Pearson English Readers series, please
visit www.pearsonenglishreaders.com. Alternatively, write to your local Pearson Education
office or to Pearson English Readers Marketing Department, Pearson Education,
Edinburgh Gate, Harlow, Essex CM20 2JE, England.

Introduction

WOMAN: What can we do? Can we stop this man?
FUERST: Perhaps we can. But first we must find a hero – a Swiss hero!

It is a bad time for Switzerland in the early 1300s. Swiss people are unhappy because their country has an Austrian emperor. There are a lot of new taxes, and there are Austrian soldiers in every town. The Swiss people want to live in *their* country, not in a new Austrian Switzerland. But what can they do? How can they fight the emperor, his governor and his soldiers? They want a hero, but where can they find one? Who can help Switzerland?

William Tell is not a soldier. He is a man of peace – a good man. Can he help his people? Is he going to fight for his country? Is he going to be Switzerland's first important hero? Or is he going to stay in the mountains, away from the fight, with his work and his family?

The German writer of this play, Friedrich von Schiller, lived from 1759 to 1805. At school, young Schiller started to write plays. He always wanted to write important stories about difficult problems in many countries. Later, he was a teacher and he was a good friend of the writer Johann Wolfgang von Goethe. Schiller never visited Switzerland. But Goethe went there and then talked to his friend about that country and its people. Schiller started to think about Switzerland and William Tell. Today, people know this Swiss hero from Schiller's play or from films of the story for television and cinema.

The People in the Play

THE SWISS

WILLIAM TELL, a hunter

HEDWIG, William Tell's wife, Walter Fuerst's daughter

WALTHER and WILHELM, William and Hedwig Tell's sons

KONRAD BAUMGARTEN

WALTER FUERST

WERNER STAUFFACHER

ARNOLD VON MELCHTAL

WERNI, a hunter

RUODI, a boatman

MAN, in Altdorf

WOMAN, in Altdorf

PEOPLE OF ALTDORF

THE AUSTRIANS

HERMANN GESSLER, an important Austrian governor
in Switzerland

SOLDIERS 1 and 2, Gessler's soldiers

BOATMAN, Gessler's boatman

Scene 1 In Altdorf, Switzerland

[*Fuerst, Stauffacher and Von Melchtal are in a street near Governor Gessler's office, near a tall, thin tree. There is a second tree across the street, and a fruit shop. Gessler is sitting in his office.*]

FUERST: This is an important day. We're going to meet with Governor Gessler. We can't be late!

STAUFFACHER: Our Austrian emperor and his governors don't understand the Swiss people. We aren't Austrians. We're Swiss and we love our country.

FUERST: And we don't want to give our money to Austria.

VON MELCHTAL: Here's one of Gessler's soldiers. It's time. Let's go in and talk. Gessler *must* understand our problems.

[*Fuerst, Stauffacher and Von Melchtal go into Governor Gessler's office. Gessler looks angry.*]

GESSLER: What do you want now? You Swiss people come here every day with a new problem.

FUERST: Our problems aren't new. You never listen to us. Things are difficult in Switzerland these days.

GESSLER: Difficult? I don't understand.

FUERST: Your soldiers are always watching us. Every day you put a new tax on us. There are taxes on our food, our houses and our animals. How can we live with these taxes?

GESSLER [*with a smile*]: Perhaps *you* can't. But *I* can live very well with them. And the Emperor is happy

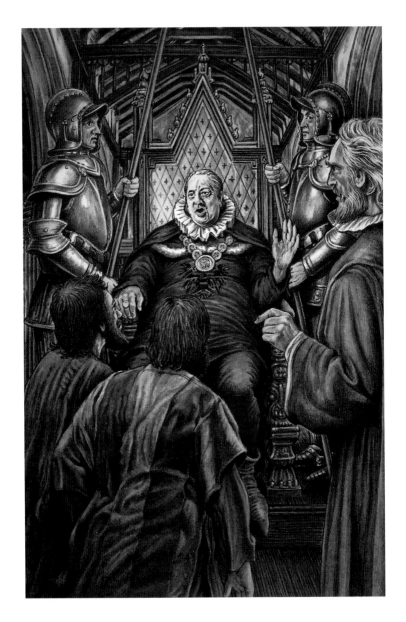

'We don't want to be Austrians. We're Swiss!'

with them too.

STAUFFACHER: But *we're* very *un*happy.

VON MELCHTAL: We don't *want* to be Austrians. We're Swiss! Please listen to us.

GESSLER: Your Austrian emperor is very good to you – but you don't understand him.

FUERST: That's right! And *he* doesn't understand *us*!

GESSLER: This is *our* country now. Go home. Listen to me and to the Emperor, or things are going to get very dangerous for every Swiss man, woman and child. Go! I don't want to talk to you. My time is important and *you* are *not*.

[*They go into the street again. People are waiting for them.*]

MAN: What did the Governor say? Is he going to send his soldiers back to Austria?

WOMAN: Is he going to stop putting taxes on us? Did he understand our problems?

FUERST: No, he didn't listen to us.

WOMAN: What can we do? Can we stop this man?

FUERST: Perhaps we can. But first we must find a hero – a Swiss hero!

Scene 2   At a river in the Swiss mountains

[*The sun is going down. Two friends, Werni and Ruodi, are standing near a river.*]

WERNI: I'm going home now. Look! It's going to rain.

RUODI: I must get my boat from the river. It's getting cold

and the water looks dangerous. Winter's coming.

WERNI: Good night, Ruodi!

RUODI: Wait! Look! Who's coming?

WERNI: I know that man. It's Konrad Baumgarten.

[*Baumgarten arrives. He is running.*]

BAUMGARTEN: Help me, my friends! Boatman, quick! Take me across the river now or I'm a dead man. Please!

RUODI: What's the problem? Who wants to kill you?

BAUMGARTEN: Gessler's men. They're coming. Quick!

RUODI: Why are they looking for you?

BAUMGARTEN: I killed one of the Governor's taxmen. I was at work, away from home. The man came to my house. He asked my wife for water – and then he wanted *her*! My wife came to me for help. I went home quickly, and then I killed him with my knife.

WERNI: You did well. Ruodi, quick! Take him across the river in your boat.

RUODI: I can't. The river's moving very quickly and the rain is heavy. No boat can go across the river now.

WERNI: Ruodi, you *must* help this man. He has a family.

RUODI: *I* have a wife and three sons too. Look at the river – it's dangerous. I want to help, but I can't.

BAUMGARTEN: Then I'm dead.

WERNI: A man is coming! Oh, it's William Tell.

[*William Tell arrives.*]

TELL: Good evening, my friends. What's wrong here?

WERNI: Baumgarten killed one of the Governor's taxmen.

'A man is coming! Oh, it's William Tell.'

The soldiers are looking for him, but our boatman can't take him across the river.

RUODI: The river's dangerous. Look at it!

TELL: But Baumgarten can't wait here. What can we do?

RUODI: There's my boat and there's the river. *You* can take the boat and be the hero. I'm going to stay here.

TELL: Baumgarten, let's go – quickly! Werni, send my love to my family.

Scene 3 At Stauffacher's home

[*Later that evening, Tell and Baumgarten are visiting Stauffacher.*]

STAUFFACHER [*to Baumgarten*]: Your story isn't new. The Emperor's governors, his Austrian soldiers *and* his taxmen make new problems for us every day.

TELL: Gessler is playing games with our country. We don't want to kill people. We don't want to fight. We're men of peace. But what can we do?

BAUMGARTEN: Let's find a number of good, strong Swiss men. We must stop these Austrians.

STAUFFACHER: I'm going to visit Walter Fuerst tomorrow. He loves our country. He can help us.

BAUMGARTEN: We must fight for our country. Let's start now!

TELL: Yes, we must help our country, but can't we find peace? I'm going home. My family are waiting. But remember – you can always ask for my help.

Scene 4 In the mountains near Tell's home

[*Gessler is on the mountain road to Altdorf with two soldiers. Tell is hunting near the road, but moves in front of Gessler.*]

TELL: Hello! You're the famous Governor Gessler. Am I right?

GESSLER: You're right – and who are you?

TELL: My name's William Tell. I'm a hunter and I'm Swiss.

GESSLER: That's interesting. But I haven't got time for you. I'm an important man with important work in Altdorf. Move!

TELL: Wait! First, we must talk. Then you can go.

GESSLER: Why do I want to talk to *you*?

TELL: Because this is my country. You're making problems for us with your taxes and your soldiers. The people of this country are very unhappy.

GESSLER: Wait! William Tell? I know about you! You helped Baumgarten.

TELL: Yes, but Baumgarten is a good man. He killed your taxman because the man was dangerous.

GESSLER: Aren't you a dangerous man too? Don't you always have a crossbow with you? Don't you go into the mountains every day and kill?

TELL: I kill animals. I put food on my family's table. I don't kill people. Can your soldiers say that?

GESSLER: I haven't got time for your talk. Move! Now!

TELL: Why? It's not late. Please listen to me. You and your taxes are bad for Switzerland. We don't want you here.

GESSLER: But I am here and I'm going to stay. This is a

7

new Switzerland and you must listen to us.

TELL: And *you* must understand the Swiss people. We love our country, our mountains and our families. We want peace – and we're going to fight for it. Watch us.

Scene 5 At William Tell's home

[*Tell and Hedwig are sitting at their table and talking.*]

HEDWIG: You're going to have problems with Gessler now.

TELL: Why? I talked to him. I didn't *hit* him.

HEDWIG: But he's going to remember you. He's going to make problems for us. Wait and see.

TELL: I'm a man of peace. I'm going to stay away from Governor Gessler now.

HEDWIG: Please do that. Where are Walther and Wilhelm?

TELL: They're in the garden. They're playing a game. Look at them. They're little soldiers.

HEDWIG: William, this isn't good. My sons aren't going to be soldiers. I want peace in my country *and* in my family.

TELL: I understand, Hedwig. Our sons are going to be hunters, but one day our country is going to want soldiers too. At that time, every man, woman and child must fight for Switzerland.

HEDWIG: William, can't you go to the Emperor? Can't you and your friends talk to *him* about peace?

TELL: Yes, we're going to try, but then …

[*Walther and Wilhelm run into the house.*]

WALTHER: Father, are we going to Altdorf now?

TELL: Yes, my son. Have you got your crossbow?

HEDWIG: Why is he taking his crossbow?

TELL: I'm a hunter. I want to teach my son about the mountains and about hunting. He's a good student.

HEDWIG: But the mountains are dangerous for a young boy.

TELL: We're mountain people. This country isn't dangerous for us. I'm going to watch Walther, and teach him.

HEDWIG: And why are you going to Altdorf?

TELL: We're going to visit your father. I want to talk to him.

HEDWIG: My father and his friends want to start a fight. Please don't go, William! You're a man of peace.

TELL: I *must* go. *I* must help Switzerland too.

HEDWIG: But Gessler's in Altdorf today. He doesn't like you. Stay at home and go tomorrow.

TELL: No, I must go today. Let's go, Walther.

HEDWIG: Walther mustn't go. Please! He can stay with me.

WALTHER: I *want* to go with Father. I want to see the town and the people.

TELL: Hedwig, he's going to be OK with me.

[*Tell and Walther go out. Hedwig and young Wilhelm stand at the door and watch them.*]

'You all love me and your emperor. Is that right?'

Scene 6 In Altdorf

[*Governor Gessler is talking to the two soldiers in his office. In the street, people are waiting near the two trees.*]

GESSLER: Switzerland has an Austrian emperor and Austrian taxes, but the Swiss people are always a problem. [*He smiles.*] What problems can I give them today?

SOLDIER 1: Give them a new tax.

GESSLER: No, there was a new tax yesterday.

SOLDIER 2: You stopped games on Saturdays and Sundays too. *And* you closed the cafés.

SOLDIER 1: You can stop all music after six o'clock in the evening.

GESSLER: Yes – very interesting. But I'm thinking.

SOLDIER 2: What? What can you do?

GESSLER: There's a tall, thin tree in front of my office. Bring me one of my old hats. Now, put the hat on the tree. Then I want to talk to the people.

[*The soldiers go into the street and put the hat on the tree. Then Gessler stands up and opens his window. The people in the street look at him.*]

GESSLER: People of Switzerland! You can see a hat on the tree in front of you. Why is it there? Can you think?

MAN: We don't know. Is it important?

GESSLER: It's *very* important to *you*. You all love me and your emperor. Is that right?

WOMAN [*quietly*]: Ha!

11

GESSLER: What did she say?

MAN [*quickly*]: She's happy. That's all.

GESSLER [*with a smile*]: You can't see *me* every day because I have a lot of important work. But you can stop every day and look at my *hat*. You can send your love to the Emperor, and to me too.

MAN [*quietly*]: Our love? How can we love a *hat*? Or the Austrians?

WOMAN [*to Gessler*]: Must we stop for your old hat?

GESSLER: Yes! All of you must stop. My soldiers are going to be here every day. They're going to watch you.

Scene 7 In front of the tree with the hat

[*Later the same day, Gessler's two soldiers are standing in the street near the tree.*]

SOLDIER 1: People aren't going to walk here.

SOLDIER 2: They don't want to stop for a hat.

SOLDIER 1: Perhaps they don't love the Emperor and his governor.

SOLDIER 2: But it's only a hat! It's not on the Emperor's head. I don't want to make problems for people.

SOLDIER 1: But this is our job. Look! A man and a boy are coming. Let's watch them.

[*William and Walther Tell come into the street. They are talking and they don't see the hat on the tree or the soldiers.*]

WALTHER: Father, does every country have tall, beautiful mountains?

'Look! A man and a boy are coming. Let's watch them.'

TELL: No, son. Switzerland is famous for its mountains. We Swiss understand them – and I'm going to teach *you*.

WALTHER: Look, Father! Why is there a hat on that tree?

TELL: I don't know, but it's not important. Let's go.

SOLDIER 1: Stop! In the name of the Emperor of Austria, stop and look up at the hat.

TELL: No. Why?

SOLDIER 1: No questions. Come with us.

TELL: What are you talking about?

SOLDIER 2: You're coming with us – to prison.

TELL: I don't understand. What's the problem here?

[*Fuerst, Stauffacher and Von Melchtal arrive. People come into the street and watch.*]

FUERST: Stop! This man is from my family. What's the problem?

SOLDIER 2: He didn't stop for the hat. He doesn't love the Emperor.

VON MELCHTAL [*to the people in the street*]: Friends, look at this! Do we want a hat on a tree in our streets? Is this an emperor? [*to the soldiers*] You can't take William Tell away. He's a man of peace.

MAN: Don't take Tell!

WOMAN [*quickly*]: The Governor is coming!

[*Gessler arrives.*]

GESSLER: Is there a problem here?

SOLDIER 1: Yes, Governor. This man and his son didn't

stop for your hat. We're taking them to prison. [*quietly*] But the people of the town are with *him*, not *us*.

TELL [*to Gessler*]: Is the hat important? I'm sorry, Governor. But there's no problem. This afternoon, tomorrow and every day I'm going to stop and look up at your hat. I want peace in Altdorf and in all of Switzerland.

GESSLER: William Tell! You're a difficult man. And you have your crossbow with you again.

WALTHER: My father can hit an apple on a tree from a hundred feet with his crossbow.

GESSLER: Can he? Soldier, bring me an apple! [*Soldier 1 takes an apple from the fruit shop and gives it to the Governor.*] Good! Tell, take your son to that tree across the street and put this apple on his head. Then take your crossbow and walk away. Hit the apple and you and your son can live.

TELL: On my son's *head*? No father can do that! Kill me now.

GESSLER: No, do it! You and your crossbow are famous. Boy, stand near the tree and wait for your father's arrow.

FUERST: Governor, stop! Take my money and my house, but don't kill Tell and Walther.

WALTHER: I'm going to be OK. [*He smiles.*] Father can hit this apple. There's no problem.

STAUFFACHER: Tell, wait! Your hand is moving and your eyes are swimming in your head. Don't play this man's games!

TELL: Governor, kill *me*, not my son.

GESSLER: I want to watch you with your crossbow. Do it!

WALTHER: Father, you can do it. I'm going to be OK.

15

[*Tell looks very unhappy. There is suddenly a lot of noise in the street. People come out of their houses because they want to watch. Tell quietly takes a second arrow from his bag and puts it in his shirt. Gessler sees him.*]

MAN: Yes, *you* can do it, Tell!

WOMAN: You're a hero!

MAN [*to the woman*]: Tell's our man!

WOMAN [*to the man*]: We don't want that hat on the tree!

GESSLER: Tell, hit the apple and go home. Look! Your son is waiting.

WALTHER: You can do it, Father.

[*People stop moving and are very quiet. Tell walks away. Then he puts an arrow in his crossbow and looks at the apple. The arrow hits the apple. The people in the street are very happy, but Tell cannot move.*]

MAN: He did it!

WALTHER: Look, Father! I'm OK – I'm not dead.

WOMAN: Every Swiss man, woman and child is going to hear about William Tell.

MAN: He's our hero! Tell can hit an apple – [*quietly*] or a soldier.

FUERST: Walther, William, let's go to my house. Come with me.

GESSLER: Stop! I want to talk to Tell.

TELL: Yes, Governor?

GESSLER: Good job, Tell. But where's your second arrow?

TELL: In my shirt.

GESSLER: Why did you *have* a second arrow?

'Look, Father! I'm OK – I'm not dead.'

TELL: It was for you – a dead governor for a dead son. But now the arrow can stay in my shirt and I can go home. Goodbye.

GESSLER: An arrow for me? Soldiers, take him to prison! He's not going to walk away from me.

MAN: No! Wait! He's a good man.

WOMAN: He's a man of peace.

MAN: He's our hero!

FUERST: You're a very bad man, Governor Gessler.

GESSLER [*to Tell*]: I'm not going to kill you, Tell, but you're dangerous. I'm going to put you in prison in Kuessnacht. I don't want you and your crossbow on these streets. Soldiers, take him to my boat.

Scene 8 On the Governor's boat

[*It is a dark night. Gessler's two soldiers are talking. Gessler's boatman is having problems with the boat.*]

SOLDIER 1: Why is Tell important to the Governor?

SOLDIER 2: He's very good with the crossbow. And he's a hero to the Swiss people. The Governor doesn't like him, but the Swiss people love him now.

SOLDIER 1: Look at this rain. It's very dangerous on the water. Where's *our* hero now. We're never going to arrive at Kuessnacht.

[*Governor Gessler comes to them.*]

GESSLER: Where's my boatman?

BOATMAN: Here I am, Governor.

GESSLER: What's wrong? When are we going to arrive?

BOATMAN: The rain's very heavy, Governor, and the water's dangerous. I'm not a strong man. I'm having problems with the boat.

GESSLER: Soldiers! Help the boatman!

BOATMAN: What do *they* know about boats?

GESSLER: Get some help! Now!

SOLDIER 1 [*slowly*]: The prisoner Tell's good with boats.

GESSLER: Bring the prisoner to me.

[*The soldiers go away, and then come back with Tell.*]

GESSLER: Tell, help us with this boat!

TELL: How can I help you? Look at me. I'm a prisoner, not a boatman.

GESSLER: You're not a prisoner now, Tell. Boatman, here's your helper.

[*Tell and the boatman work on the boat. After some time, the boat gets to Kuessnacht.*]

GESSLER: Here we are! Soldiers! Take Tell to the prison.

TELL: What? Prison? No! I'm going to take my crossbow and say goodbye.

[*Tell quickly takes his crossbow and runs away from the boat into the dark night.*]

SOLDIER 1: Where did he go?

SOLDIER 2 [*with a smile*]: He helped *us* and now he's going to help his people. He *is* a hero.

'But I *can see* you!'

GESSLER: Stop him! In Altdorf, he wanted to kill me.
SOLDIER 1: But we can't see him.
TELL [*from the road*]: But *I* can see *you*!

[*Tell takes the second arrow from his shirt and puts it in his crossbow. The arrow hits Governor Gessler in the head. Gessler falls. Tell runs away.*]

SOLDIER 1: Oh, no! The Governor's dead!
SOLDIER 2: Where's Tell?
SOLDIER 1: He's in the mountains now. We can never find him. Let's take our dead governor to his house in Kuessnacht.

Scene 9 In a street in Altdorf

[*William Tell arrives in the town. He meets Fuerst and Von Melchtal there, in the street.*]

FUERST: William! You're back! How did you get away from Gessler and his soldiers?
TELL: I helped them with their boat on a very bad night. Then I killed the Governor.
VON MELCHTAL: Yes! Now things are going to be good again in our country.
FUERST: Gessler's dead, but we must finish Tell's work. We must send the Austrians back to their home.
VON MELCHTAL: Let's start our fight today. Tell, you're our hero. Can you help us again?
TELL: Of course I can. Every Swiss person is going to fight for their country. Many years from now, our children's

21

children are going to talk about our fight.

[*A man runs to them, with Gessler's hat in his hands. A woman walks into the street too.*]

MAN [*to the woman*]: Here's Gessler's hat.
WOMAN: What can we do with *that*? Do we want it?
MAN: Put it in the river. Send it to Austria!
TELL: Wait! Let's put it in an important place. Let's look at it every day and remember Gessler. Let's say, 'Never again! Switzerland is for the Swiss.'
FUERST [*to Tell*]: But isn't the Emperor going to look for you? Isn't he going to come here with his soldiers?
TELL: Yes, Gessler was his friend and one of his governors. But we're strong and we can stop the soldiers. We can wait for them in the mountains.
MAN: We must listen to William Tell.
VON MELCHTAL: You're right. But wait! Who's coming? It's Stauffacher.

[*Stauffacher runs to them.*]

STAUFFACHER: Listen! The Emperor is dead!
FUERST: What? How?
VON MELCHTAL: When?
STAUFFACHER: Many *Austrian* people didn't like Gessler or the Emperor. The Emperor was on the road to Baden, here in Switzerland. Some Austrians stopped him and killed him. Then they went back to Austria.
FUERST: This *is* a good day for our country. Now we've got an important job. We must build a strong

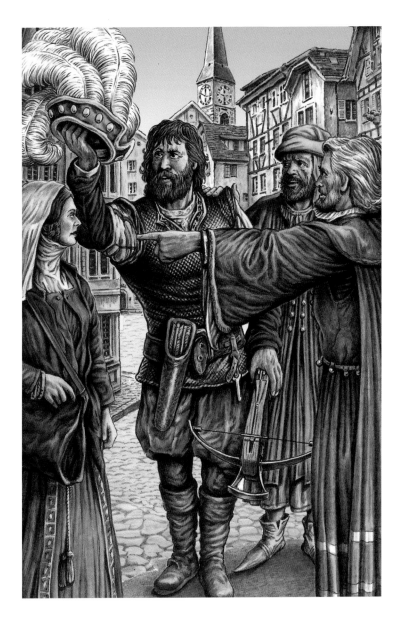

'Let's say, "Never again! Switzerland is for the Swiss."'

Switzerland.

TELL: We can have peace now. Goodbye, my friends. I'm going home – to the mountains and to my family.

VON MELCHTAL: Thank you, William. Switzerland is always going to remember you.

ALL: You're our hero, William Tell!

ACTIVITIES

Scenes 1–3

Before you read

1 Where is Switzerland? What do you know about this country and its people?

2 You are going to read about William Tell. He is a famous Swiss hero. Do you know the names of some famous heroes from your country? Talk about their stories.

3 Look at the Word List at the back of the book. Then answer these questions.

    a Which five words are for people?

    b How often do you eat an apple? Why?

    c Are people usually happy about a lot of taxes? Why (not)?

    d Who helps students with problems at your school?

    e Where can people hunt in your country?

    f Are the roads near your house dangerous? Why (not)?

    g Do good people go to prison?

While you read

4 Who is it? Write the names.

    a He is an Austrian governor in Switzerland. ....………

    b He wants to find a hero for Switzerland. ....………

    c He is running from Gessler's men. ....………

    d He is a boatman, but he doesn't like to be on the water in heavy rain. ....………

    e He helps Konrad Baumgarten. ....………

    f He talks to Baumgarten and Tell in his house. ....………

After you read

5 Talk to a friend. Are these sentences right or wrong?

    a This is an unhappy time for the Swiss people.

    b Gessler wants to be Swiss.

    c Austrian soldiers and taxes are problems for the Swiss.

d Konrad Baumgarten's wife is dead.

e William Tell wants peace for his country.

f Stauffacher, Baumgarten and Tell want to be Austrian soldiers.

Scenes 4–6

Before you read

6 What are you going to read about now? What do you think? Talk about these questions.

    a Are Governor Gessler and William Tell going to be friends?

    b Which Swiss men are going to fight for their country?

    c Who *isn't* going to want to fight?

While you read

7 Who is it? Put a tick (√) in the right places.

	Tell	Hedwig	Gessler	Walther
a works in Altdorf				
b always has a crossbow with him				
c kills animals for food for his family				
d doesn't understand Swiss people				
e wants to know about the mountains				
f wants Walther at home				
g likes making problems for Swiss people				
h has an old hat on a tree				

After you read

8 Work with a friend.

    Student A: You are Walther Tell. You are walking to Altdorf with your father. Ask questions about the mountains, about hunting and about your country's problems.

    Student B: You are William Tell. Answer your son's questions.

Scenes 7–9

Before you read

9 Talk about Governor Gessler's hat.

    a Why is it important to the Austrian governor and his soldiers?

    b What do the Swiss people think about it?

    c Is the hat going to bring peace or problems to Switzerland?

While you read

10 What comes first? Write the numbers 1–8.

    a William Tell helps Gessler's boatman in the heavy rain. …..

    b William Tell goes to his family home and his country has peace again. …..

    c Governor Gessler sees his soldiers with Tell and his son. …..

    d William Tell kills Gessler. …..

    e The Austrian soldiers stop William Tell and his son. …..

    f The Austrian soldiers take William Tell to Gessler's boat. …..

    g William Tell's arrow hits the apple on Walther's head. …..

    h Some Austrian men kill the Emperor. …..

After you read

11 Why are these important in the story? Talk about them.

    a the Governor's hat

    b the Austrian soldiers

    c Tell's crossbow

    d an apple

    e Tell's second arrow

f heavy rain

g the dead Emperor

Writing

12 You are the Austrian emperor. Write a letter to Governor Gessler at the start of his job in Altdorf. He must work for Austria, not Switzerland.

13 You are Walther Tell. You are going to go home after your visit to Altdorf. What are you going to say to your brother and mother? Write your story first.

14 Gessler and the Austrian emperor are dead. The Austrian soldiers go home. What are the people of Altdorf going to do this weekend, in the new Switzerland? Write about it.

15 Write a newspaper story about Switzerland's new hero, William Tell.

16 Write a scene from the play after William Tell kills his son with the arrow from his crossbow. What does he say? What does he do?

17 Did you like this play about William Tell? Is it interesting or not? Why? Write about the play.